A Communal Cure: How to Heal Our EDUCATIONAL SYSTEM'S Sickness

VOLUME 1

A Communal Cure: How to Heal Our EDUCATIONAL SYSTEM'S Sickness

VOLUME 1

PROFESSOR OUELE

Library of Congress Control Number: 2023918962

ISBN: 978-1-960093-41-7   (Paperback)
ISBN: 978-1-960093-42-4   (eBook)

Printed in the United States of America

DEDICATION

This book is dedicated to all teachers around the world. They work tirelessly to educate students, week in, week out, sometimes even on weekends. Anyone in society is the product of teachers.

Acknowledgements

I want to express my gratitude to my family, who supported me during the process of writing this book. I also want to thank all teachers who encouraged me to move forward and complete this book.

Contact: connect@professorouele.com

Introduction

The state of health of a country's education system gives an idea of the economic and political health of the country. Many countries that have understood this are emphasizing the improvement of their education systems. When education is sick, it is as if the whole system is sick. To say today that education is in bad shape is not an exaggeration. What is taught to students today and the merits of how it is taught are debatable. The quality of education is declining; teachers lack motivation and leave their profession, and it is not easy to find their replacements. Students seem to have lost interest in school for several reasons: the levels of violence on campus are becoming unacceptable, and the students and their families do not approve of what is imposed on them in the classroom, which is often not in line with daily reality. Further, politics dictates what education should be, which is often not accepted by students, parents, and teachers. The COVID-19 pandemic worsened the situation.

The multiple issues that are ruining the education system worldwide inspired me to write this book. I have a Ph.D. in education, and I've been teaching since 1992 at almost all levels and in several countries — positioning me as an expert in this field. In this, Volume 1, I perform an autopsy of the educational system and name some issues that undermine it through Part 1, as well as some practices in Part 2 to remedy the illness befalling our students.

I do not claim to have developed all the concepts in this book. References for research cited can be found in the back. I hope that my modest contribution can be taken into consideration by the actors of education, in particular the students, teachers, and families as well as the decision makers. I believe that strong and immediate action must be taken to avoid the worst outcome for a society of inadequately educated people.

PREFACE

Our education system is broken. Many students go from class to class without having the appropriate level of prerequisites. Many students have missed portions of their intended learning and complete their studies with a lot of gaps. The COVID-19 pandemic highlights the failing education system. As the pandemic wanes, it feels like there is a dip in enthusiasm from teachers, students, and parents. All seem to need moral support.

The pandemic has exposed the shortcomings of the education system. The education system is broken in various ways. The pandemic has made the situation worse. Research indicates that the pandemic has put students two years behind, academically. The first part of this book highlights the challenges facing the education system. The second part of the book provides some recommendations for solving these problems.

Table of Contents

PART 1

OVERVIEW OF THE CURRENT EDUCATIONAL SYSTEM

The education system is sick. The problems that undermine it are multiple.

CHAPTER 1
Our educational system is broken

The system of education is broken for various reasons, including the following.

SHORTAGE OF TEACHERS

There is a shortage of teachers. In many parts of the world, the shortage is nationwide. The situation is so serious that some school districts are forced to recruit candidates who do not have sufficient qualifications. Imagine someone in the classroom with no license and no knowledge of the subject they are teaching. You may think it is a joke, but it is commonplace these days.

The following are some causes of the teacher shortage. I believe COVID-19 took the lives of many unfortunate teachers. Through the initial pandemic, many teachers were at home. However, as doors began opening once again across the world, teachers joined nurses and medical teams in consistent daily exposure.

In addition, the number of teachers who resign is increasingly high because they are poorly paid and most of the time work in unacceptable conditions. I asked a one-question survey to 50 of my students: would you like to become a teacher when you grow up? Surprisingly, all of them said no. This made me suspect that the teacher shortage we are facing today may continue if nothing is done to solve the problem. Some schools are closing for lack of teachers. Teachers who remain are overworked. Classes are being combined, and therefore, often overcrowded. It is obvious that the increase in the number of students and the decrease in teachers negatively affects the teacher/student ratio. The number of students per teacher is increasing. In various countries, one K–12 teacher has 50 to 80 students. In such a situation, what are we expecting from that teacher? They have to prepare the lessons, struggle to manage the classroom, and grade students' work — sometimes after hours or over the weekend — without compensation for overtime.

The rate of absenteeism among teachers is becoming worrying: depending on the size of the school, there are schools where 15 to 20 teachers are absent on the same day. The high absenteeism rate may reflect the hostile environment in which teachers work, or just fatigue on their part. It is well known that employees who are not treated well at their workplace tend to be absent. Unfortunately, there are not enough substitute teachers.

It is important to mention that there are two categories of teachers: the first group is made up of teachers who work out of love for their vocation and their profession. The second group includes individuals who find themselves in teaching by accident: they find themselves in teaching because they have not found anything better elsewhere.

They don't have love for what they do. They just put in enough effort to keep their job. Unfortunately, the number of teachers who find themselves in the second category is increasing alarmingly.

STANDARDIZED TESTING

In the early 21st century, American teachers were required to implement the Common Core standard — a nearly nationwide general education curriculum — leaving little room for them to innovate. One of the intentions of Common Core was to support students in completing high school with the ability to compete with other students around the world. The advantage of Common Core was that it assisted teachers in teaching the content and subjects with all the same guidelines. This made it easier for students to transition from one grade or school to another because the instruction would be identical. However, many teachers viewed Common Core as the interference of government in education. It prevented each state from using its own test or adjusting the instruction according to the local reality.

The implementation of the Common Core also meant the assessment of students in the United States with the standardized state achievement tests. Unfortunately, preparing students for standardized tests takes a lot of instructional time. Moreover, the tests' outcomes do not always reflect reality; for example, an intelligent student who is going through some health or family issues, or who is hungry or stressed out, may perform poorly.

It is not fair to use standardized tests to assess teachers because students are not necessarily tested on what they were taught. Those tests focus mostly on English and math. They do not evaluate critical thinking or students' ability to solve a problem.

Students take the standardized tests at almost the end of the school year. The result of those tests are released over the summer, when students are on break. Although students' families do receive the test scores, the information is not intended to benefit any of those students' educational outcome. These tests assist the Education Department in remediating low-scoring schools, which goes into effect at a later time. It would be better if the results of these tests could be used to support students.

In addition, the origin of standardized testing has a connection with racism: Rosales and Walker (2021) found that standardized testing was a tool for racism. Those suffering from it are students of color or those from low-income families. Kendi (2020) also indicated that standardized tests are an efficient racist weapon, aimed at denying Black and Brown students entry to renowned schools.

POLITICS OVERSHADOWING EDUCATION

Politicians dictate what education should be. They have said no student must fail. That concept hurts more than helps students: each and every year, regardless of their academic performance, students are moved to the next level. What is sad is that some students are completing high school without being able to write a well-structured paragraph. Their sentences are full of errors. They cannot read or write properly.

Many students are left behind. Politicians are telling teachers indirectly that if they try all options to support a student and do not see any improvement, they should just give the student a good grade and let them move forward. That is another indication of the failure of the educational system. In various school districts, students and their families have the right to contest a grade. They are so powerful that they can urge the school, with or without reason, to change the grade; it is becoming common, more evidence that the system has failed. The direct consequence is that many students graduate undeservedly.

SOCIAL MEDIA

Social media is now considered a weapon of mass distraction for everyone, especially for students. The most vulnerable groups are middle and high school students. In class, while the teachers strive to teach, these students are on YouTube, Instagram, Facebook, TikTok, and so on. Others are playing games on their cell phones. Some insult the teacher outright when the teacher asks them to stop using their electronic devices. Quite often, parents get involved, feeling that their children should have access to electronic devices and should be reachable at all times by telephone; this makes the work of the school staff more complicated.

Those students also have access to forbidden websites. When the teacher comes next to them, they flip the page they were watching. The development of technology leads to cheating and alters learning. Students can easily cheat with their cell phone. During the instruction, some parents are communicating with their children via phone calls or text messages. So as not to lose the messages, these students hold their telephone in their hand or keep it under the table. They are distracted and uninterested in what the teacher is teaching. What is disturbing is that some families are part of the issue: they spoil their children by giving them more than what they need. Just for communication, does an elementary school student need the latest version of a smartphone?

VIOLENCE IN SCHOOLS

Insecurity in schools is a serious concern for parents, students, and teachers. Violence in school is on the rise. This violence takes many forms, including fighting, bullying, and shooting.

Quite often, when you tune in the radio or television, you hear that in schools there are shootings that killed or injured students. In some schools, the police are present to deter criminals; however, we have cases where students evade security, enter the school building and kill their classmates with guns. While one assassin breaks into a school in Texas and kills multiple students and staff members, in Virginia a six-year-old student arrives on his campus and shoots his teacher. The lack of security is a serious problem in schools. I previously mentioned the shortage of teachers. How many potential teachers are willing to accept teaching positions and to get hurt or shot by students or someone else?

Several school districts instituted the lockdown drill to prepare students for the event of a shooting. Some questions to ask are: Why does someone take away the lives of innocent students and teachers with a gun? What triggered the problem? Why do we have guns in the hands of the wrong people? It is sad to see innocent children losing their lives on the way to learning. Today, students are traumatized; they are afraid to go to school. Families are afraid to send their children to school.

When there is a mass shooting, politicians give speeches without taking action. They are quick to connect the shooting to mental illnesses, which in turn leads to conversations about gun owners regularly undergoing mental evaluation. What can be said about the shooting is that if we don't control the gun, the gun will control us.

Secondly, fighting in schools is becoming a worrying problem. Very often, it all starts with inappropriate jokes that end in fights. The school law does not allow teachers to intervene between students fighting. What teachers are told to do is call school officials for intervention. The intervention sometimes arrives late; in the meantime, students hurt themselves or others and destroy school property. The fight traumatizes students; it prevents them from focusing on the instruction because they think that at any moment another fight may begin. The issue is so serious that some students are forced to miss classes or drop out of school because they are afraid of being beaten up by their classmates.

At school dismissal each day, the probability of a fight is very high. Students who were compressed all day let off steam. They do not control their energy. They challenge each other to a fight. The presence of police may be helpful, but we cannot have police in all schools.

The third issue is bullying. This section will provide a definition of bullying and explain some types of bullying as well as how it affects students. Some strategies to handle bullying will be explained in the second part of the book. Rigby (2007) indicated that "Bullying is repeated oppression, psychological or physical, of a less powerful person by a more powerful person or group of persons" (p.15). From this definition, we can infer that for the bullying to occur there should be at least two persons, and one person or group of persons is stronger than the other person or group. In addition, the abuse must be repeated. Olweus (1994) stated: "A student is being bullied or victimized when he or she is exposed, repeatedly and over time, to negative actions on the part of one or more other students" (p. 9).

The groups most at risk of being bullied are minority groups with certain physical characteristics; we can cite, among others, disabled and obese people. As a physically disabled person, I was the victim of bullying at school: my classmates regularly provoked me and made fun of my disability, they imitated the way I walked, and they used sobriquets to insult me.

Bullying in schools is a growing concern for parents, families, students, and teachers. This happens in class during the lessons, at dismissal, and even at home. It takes various forms: verbal, social, physical, and cyber. Using racist words to describe a person, disrespect, name calling, and insults are forms of verbal bullying. Pushing, kicking, or hitting someone is part of physical bullying. Dishonoring someone by lying, spreading false information, or making inappropriate jokes are considered social bullying. Juvoneni & Graham (2014) indicated that cyberbullying encompasses using cell phones to send text messages and posting messages on social media. Social media promotes violence. Students now have easy access to computers or cell phones. Those electronic devices are an open door to various social media. Social media is also a serious distraction for students: some of them fake that they need to use the restroom; when the teacher allows them to go, they spend valuable instructional time in the restroom on their phone, sometimes accessing prohibited websites.

GROWING POVERTY

Poverty is becoming a serious concern almost everywhere. Students from poor families are coming to school without eating. Not all schools have a free lunch program. Hungry students do not focus or even sleep during the instruction. Starving students can get sick; this also means that they may miss days of school. Starvation impacts students' academic performance. Moreover, poor families may not be able to buy school supplies.

LACK OF STATE FUNDING FOR SCHOOLS

Some countries are doing what they can by putting at the disposal of schools almost everything they need. But in various parts of the world, the funding of education is not a priority. Governments have money for war but nothing for education. The purchase of school supplies is entirely the responsibility of the parents, who are often without means. Tuition fees can be very expensive and beyond the reach of poor families. In several poor or badly organized countries, school is fee-based, from elementary school to university, which limits the chances of children from poor families having access to education. Students do not have access to computers or the internet and are therefore technologically behind. Some countries make buses available to students for transportation from home to school and back. Some poor countries do not have this privilege; destitute students travel a very long distance every day to get to school.

Some wealthier countries offer breakfast and lunch to students for free or at greatly reduced rates. In several other poor countries, each student comes to school with their own food. Some of them come to school without food, for lack of means.

LACK OF FAMILIES' INVOLVEMENT

From my experience teaching, I have seen that many parents and guardians are not involved enough in their students' education. Some parents have transferred all responsibility to teachers. They think teachers will do everything for their children. They don't support their kids at home and don't check if homework is done. Some of these parents don't even ask their children what they learned in school.

Once at home, all the children have to do is watch television or play games for hours and go to bed very late.

Most students who have not slept enough at night sleep in class during instruction. Some poor parents are forced to work two jobs. They come home when their children are asleep and go to work early in the morning when the children are still asleep. Left to fend for themselves, these children miss classes or arrive late for school, often with nothing to eat. Under these conditions, what performance can we expect from these students?

INSUFFICIENT SUPPORT FOR STUDENTS WITH DISABILITIES

Many countries have legislation protecting students with disabilities. The issue is in the implementation of that legislation. In the 21st century, some countries still ignore the needs of the disabled community. Students with disabilities attend classes without any accommodations. Nobody cares about their specific needs. In such a difficult environment, students with disabilities drop out of school early.

As a disabled person, I went to school in a very difficult situation: I couldn't walk. Every day, my brothers carried me on their backs for long distances due to lack of a wheelchair and no means of transport. I was placed in the same setting as the other students, without specialized teaching, without extra time to complete my assignments. What motivated me not to give up was the sacrifice of my brothers for me, as well as the constant encouragement I received from my father.

LACK OF FOCUS ON GIFTED AND TALENTED STUDENTS

The concept of gifted and talented education is still ignored by various school districts around the world. This section will provide the definition of gifted and talented, explain the difference between gifted students and other students, and explore how to identify them and the issues they face.

Various research is now available about gifted and talented students: the New Jersey Administrative Code for the Gifted (2020) defined gifted and talented students as "students who possess or demonstrate high level of ability, in one or more content areas, when compared to their chronological peers in the local school district and who require modifications of their educational program if they are to achieve in accordance with their capabilities" (New Jersey Department of Education [NJDOE], 2020).

The outcome of research conducted by Shurkin (1992) mentioned Terman as the pioneer of gifted education.

There is a difference between gifted and talented children and other children: the natural abilities of gifted and talented children exceed those of other students. They can decode concepts outside other students' understanding. In most cases, they are very curious, they are problem solvers, and they learn fast, with no need for repetition. They are high achievers.

There is no standard process to identify gifted and talented children. The method varies from school district to school district or from country to country. What is common is that all methods start with screening of students who display some potential of gifted and talented.

Administrators who administer the test must be certified. The test includes two components: the cognitive and the non-cognitive. One of the tests used to identify gifted and talented students is the Stanford-Binet Intelligence Scales. Some schools criticized past measures known as intelligence quotient (IQ) tests because they did not provide the whole information about the student's ability.

The issues with gifted and talented students are similar to those of students with disabilities. In most cases, they are mixed in the same classroom with other students and receive the same instruction instead of individualized instruction, which is bad. When they are placed in the wrong environment, they can display some misbehavior and frustrations. Some of those students are impatient. They want to be in control. They may struggle to make and keep friends because they feel they are superior to other students and find it difficult to socialize with them. Some of them also struggle with testing because they overthink; they want to be perfect. They can get bored easily, especially when they are not kept busy. The general education teachers should not teach those students without additional training. Gifted and talented students who are not in the proper setting may drop out of school early. They must be in a program that matches their needs.

INCREASING RATE OF STUDENTS DROPPING OUT

The number of students who are dropping out of school without completing their education is alarming. The U.S. Department of Education, National Center for Education Statistics (2021) indicated that in 2019, 2.0

million students between 16 and 24 years of age dropped out of school: that is, 5% of all students. By ethnicity, the dropout percentage of all students breaks down as follows:

- Caucasian — 4.1%
- Mixed-background of two or more ethnicities — 5.1%
- Black — 5.6%
- Hispanic — 7.7%
- Pacific Islander — 8.0%
- Native — 9.6%

Students drop out of school for various reasons: for example, some want to take care of their family member who is sick, but others do not find any interest in school and dislike it. Some do not like what is happening in school, such as bullying, violence, shootings, and the disconnection of the school program with real-life development. Others abandon school because they become pregnant.

INCREASED ABSENTEEISM RATE

The number of students who are coming late to school or who are absent from school is worrying. Typical causes of absence include doctor appointments, family emergencies, observance of religious events, and bad weather. Other causes of absence I stated already are bullying and violence in school. Students who are bullied or experience violence at school do not hesitate to miss classes when they can.

Truancy is a problem. There is no standard definition of truancy. However, many school districts have agreed that it is considered truancy when, without a parent's permission or knowledge, a student is absent from school for more than eight days within a quarter or fifteen days within a semester or twenty days within a school year. Truants commonly meet at a specific location during school hours to drink alcohol or consume drugs. When they abuse controlled substances, they sometimes vandalize property, steal, and commit other crimes. Some are exposed to prostitution. The main consequence of truancy is dropping out of school.

As I continue teaching, I see something becoming common. Some students, especially females, choose a school day to go to a salon to get their hair or their nails done. It is also common for students to decide to stay home on their birthday and miss the instruction.

NO CORRELATION BETWEEN THE SCHOOL PROGRAM AND REAL LIFE

Public school teachers are often slaves to the curriculum: for each subject, they teach the pre-established chapters. Nothing is planned to teach students techniques for success in their social lives. The system seems to teach us that we must go to school, study, earn degrees, and find good jobs, which is not always true. Many students finish their studies with diplomas but receive no preparation to succeed in practical life. The education system has failed to serve those aspiring to business or self-employment. A student goes from primary school to secondary school, sometimes to university, without being exposed to the reality of practical life; that is a failure. From elementary school and onward, I believe students should be exposed to training in their fields of interest.

The school system should be redesigned so that students approximate working in the real world. General education must be redesigned to integrate concrete notions. Instead of stuffing students' heads with useless theories, we must get down to business: a lesson on adding and subtracting money must be done in a real or fictitious store. A field trip can be an opportunity to teach students the measurement of distance using real tools to practice. It is useless for a student to have a bachelor's or master's degree when they know practically nothing about their field. Current school practices seem to essentially train the future unemployed. Today, it is common to see students with a master's degree doing work that has nothing to do with their studies because the reality of the field is different from school theory. Anyone who has a master's degree in economics and works as a taxi driver is not fulfilling their educational journey — and I would consider them unemployed.

MENTAL HEALTH

By mental health, I refer to the absence of any health issue that impacts the psychological or emotional well-being of an individual. Someone with a mental health issue may display some of the following characteristics: They may hear voices that nobody else can hear. They may lose hope, change their mood quickly, or struggle to sleep. They may feel isolated and hopeless. They may have suicidal thoughts or struggle to undertake daily chores.

They may perceive something that does not exist and consider it real.

Gillett (2022) researched mental health. Based on his research, the World Health Organization estimated that about 300 million people around the world are suffering from depression, and that every 40 seconds depression drives someone to commit suicide.

Before the pandemic, many parents, students, and teachers suffered from mental problems that often went unnoticed. They could display behavioral problems without them attracting anyone's attention.

The pandemic made the situation worse. To prevent the spread of the pandemic, governments around the world decided to close almost everything, including schools. Everyone was in lockdown mode except for essential workers. Even those lucky enough to have a home with four walls were isolated from other friends and family, which triggered mental health issues in many people. When students returned to school in person, those familiar with diagnostics of mental health could easily notice through some students' behavior that some of them displayed serious problems.

Mental health issues impact students in various ways: as stated, students with such issues may have suicidal thoughts or commit suicide; they feel lonely, depressed, and lack focus. Mental health negatively impacts students' academic performance.

Anyone going through a mental health challenge should seek help from doctors or counselors. It is a disease just like others. Nobody should be ashamed about it. Unfortunately, even people who begin treatment for mental health issues may drop out, whether or not it's meeting their needs, because they do not want to be labeled.

GRADUATING INTO THE AMERICAN STUDENT LOAN CRISIS

American student loans are another illustration of the failure of the educational system. We grew up learning that you must go to school, obtain the highest degree, find a well-paid job, and have a nice lifestyle. This is true, but not in all cases. What is usually not explained is how you complete your education.

In the United States, school is free from the elementary to high school levels in public institutions. Most of those students stop after high school and find a job. In college, the tuition becomes very expensive and not affordable for poor students. Students without means who want to continue with their education have two options: they can work full-time to pay for their tuition or apply for student loans. A loan, whether public or private, is not free. The reality is that many students are struggling to pay back their debt. If you borrow more than what you can repay, then you become the slave of the lender. You can be broke for the rest of your life because of the student loan debt. If for example you accumulate $300,000 of debt by the end of your education, the monthly minimum payment will be around $2,400. If we do not consider other expenses such as utility bills or food and estimate just $2,000 for the rent, how much will you earn to live a decent life? Can you easily buy a car? Can you have enough money to get married? The economic crisis is serious, and finding a well-paid job is challenging. Scott-Clauton (2018) indicated that the student loan crisis is serious. He found that Black students are five times at risk of defaulting on payment compared to white students. Some students are so broke at the end of their education that to avoid paying the rent, they return to their parents' home.

At the time of this writing, research indicated that the American student loan debt is about $1.635 trillion[1] — which exceeds the credit card and the auto loan debt. With the pandemic, the government put a pause on the repayment of student loans. But what happens if you cannot repay your student loan? If you fail to make your student loan payments, your loan will go into default. You will be reported to the credit bureau. This will affect your credit. With bad credit, you cannot be issued a credit card. You cannot buy a house or a car. Your tax refund will be held to pay your debt. Your salary can be garnished; in other words, your employer will be asked to take a portion of your salary to pay your debt. Your lender can take you to court. What is important to know is that even if you eventually pay off all your debt, your delinquent status will still show on your credit report for about seven years although the balance is zero.

As an institution, the student loan has some impacts on the economy. One of the positive impacts is that it boosts the economy, if paid. It has some negative impacts

---

[1]   Hanson, Melanie. "Student Loan Debt Statistics" EducationData. org, April 1, 2023

on the economy: it makes it difficult for the borrower to launch a business because their focus is on the repayment of their debt. The consequence is that there are fewer jobs created, which leads to a slow economy. The debt may decrease the borrower's spending. It does not allow the borrower to save. It may create a racial gap: as I mentioned above, people of color experience more financial struggles to complete their education compared to whites.

Overall, the student loan debt is a burden for the borrowers. The debate today is whether student loans, as society currently knows them, must be canceled — and how the issue can be fixed. The second part of this book will provide some suggestions.

Chapter 2
How the pandemic made the situation worse

It is December 2019. TV channels and radio stations are announcing a new deadly disease. It is the coronavirus. Corona in the morning, corona at noon, corona in the evening. In a matter of days, this word has become the most frequently spoken word. We are told it is in China. Some images that escaped from China let us see hundreds of deaths. It's scary, it's horrible. It was believed that evil was circumscribed in China. Unfortunately, no.

A few weeks later, we are informed that the disease has already spread throughout the world. In France, people are dying. In the United States, people are dying. In Italy, we no longer count the dead. Whites die. Blacks die. Young people die. The seniors die. Death becomes commonplace. No one is safe. The world suddenly turns into a house of mourning. The state of emergency is decreed. The world is closing in on itself. Schools and stores are closed. In the sky, no plane is flying over. The streets are empty. Only a few vehicles of essential workers circulate.

What is happening? people are wondering. Will it pass quickly like the blowing wind? The world is in total confusion. Scientists and politicians are taking action without reversing the disease. On the contrary, with each passing day, the disease spreads like wildfire. They tell us about variants. Each variant that arrives becomes more deadly than the previous one.

WHAT DO PEOPLE SAY ABOUT CORONA?

Years before the pandemic, several medical encyclopedias had already described corona as similar to a common cold. Many people claimed that corona is not new. The controversy over this terminology has forced scientists to use the term COVID-19 instead of corona. Other people said corona is 666, the sign of the beast: when you add each letter of the word corona you have 666:

C	=	3 (3rd letter of the alphabet)
O	=	17 (17th letter of the alphabet)
R	=	18
O	=	15
N	=	14
A	=	1
6	=	66

Other people say that corona is a handmade disease. They say that the virus escaped from a lab in China. Some even call it the Chinese virus. Investigations into the real origin of the virus are inconclusive.

After the development of the vaccine, vaccination became one of the most controversial aspects of this pandemic. The world is now divided into two: the world of vaccinated and the world of unvaccinated. On one hand, we have the government suggesting, encouraging, and forcing people to get vaccinated. Politicians and scientists said that a fully vaccinated person is someone who took two doses of vaccine. Then they said the population needed the boost. Some people took the first, second, and even third boost. Then came the confusion: what is meant by "fully vaccinated"?

On the other hand, we have some people who refused the vaccine, saying that the vaccine mandate violates their rights. Some people lost their jobs because they did not want the vaccine. They moved to some areas where rules were less rigid. They said it is not a vaccine but an experimental injection. In some parts of the world, only those who showed a so-called vaccine passport had access to restaurants and public places. Some people called it apartheid. Those who were against it were protesting. In some cases, they were brutalized by the police. Protesters said that there should not be one solution for all — especially without any alternative solutions or treatments. They pointed an accusing finger at Big Pharma, complaining that its main goal was to make money. Critics went further by saying that it may be cheaper to make medicine than vaccines and that focusing only on vaccines is not acceptable because people could have been saved with proper medication.

Other people slam the powerful countries by saying that they spend billions of dollars to know what is going on around the world and on all the planets, but they are not able to see a pandemic coming. They suspect that the world is still not prepared for a future pandemic.

Many African countries claimed that they have the cure for the pandemic. Madagascar, a small island nation in Africa, reportedly used natural medication to cure its population. That approach does not please the World Health Organization. But the reality is that Africa is the continent that has had less death from corona. Many countries in Africa did not really close down; wearing masks there was optional. The population there did not worry about social distancing.

THE PANDEMIC AND EDUCATION

The pandemic has various consequences in almost all areas: The economy has suffered from it. The unemployment rate is at its peak. Many people lost their jobs, and their houses, and became homeless.

The pandemic negatively impacted the educational system in various ways: many great teachers died of the pandemic and could not easily be replaced. I personally knew some wonderful teachers who are no longer with us because of COVID-19. They had a lot of dedication for their job. They were always the first to come to school and the last to leave the school building. Sometimes, I wondered if they really had a family life. After their death, surely the school system hired new teachers. But none of them were close to those teachers. That is why I mentioned that they could not easily be replaced.

The pandemic made one think of the fabled apocalypse which was to exterminate everyone. This created trauma and demotivation among many people, especially teachers, students, and parents.

In many parts of the world, schools were closed with no instruction at all. Some schools offered virtual learning. But it was almost a waste of time. Students did not really learn. The change of setting destroyed students' routine: they would previously wake up in the morning, take their shower, have their breakfast, and go to school. By staying home, they showed that they did not take their education seriously. It was a challenge for teachers to manage students online. Those students could turn off their cameras and play their games during instruction. Some of them took the class in their bed in their pajamas. Although they were at home, some students refused to turn on their computer to go to their classroom. Most of them could not complete their homework. Overall, students displayed a lack of interest in school during the pandemic. Research shows that the pandemic has put students two years behind. Can we make up for this delay?

Chapter 3
How schools handled the pandemic

Corona took almost everybody by surprise. A state of emergency was declared. Schools reacted differently. In many poor countries, schools were closed for almost a year with no instruction, as I mentioned already. The school districts in those countries had no means and were powerless. In other parts of the world, school districts provided computers and internet connections to students. By so doing, they enabled students to continue with their education.

School districts trained teachers in other ways to move forward with the instruction; they came up with various ideas. They used hybrid synchronous and asynchronous systems. A synchronous system means that students from their house connect themselves to their classroom using a video conferencing (aka Zoom) link. The teacher teaches them as if they were in the real classroom. With the asynchronous system, instructions and assignments are recorded and posted online. Students can join the class when they want and complete their assignments at their own pace.

Even with these adjustments, shutdown was a painful moment for parents, students, and teachers. Students did not easily get used to the new routine. Waking up, getting ready, and staying in front of the computer to learn from home made them feel like something was missing: their real classroom with their classmates. They did not have the motivation to learn. Some of them would come on the screen with no interest in the class. Others had the camera off and went back to sleep or were not participating in the instruction.

Parents who were mostly at home because of the shutdown struggled to keep their child focused on the instruction. Their challenges increased when they had two or more children to monitor at the same time. Some parents disturbed the class, just like students. What was unpleasant was that some of those parents appeared on the screen undressed or not dressed appropriately. Some students, as mentioned above, had the camera off and were not participating in the instruction. They were playing games on YouTube and on various social media. Some teachers were able to take a snapshot of those students' screens and forwarded it to their parents. Most students didn't do their homework. They procrastinated. Parents were doing their children's work. If parents were not available, students' siblings would complete the assignments and submit them. Many students received grades of 100, but that did not reflect their real performance. Some parents believed that teachers transferred to them the power of education.

School districts came with various ideas to handle the pandemic, but they had no control over the outcome. Overall, students did not really learn during the pandemic. Managing students, especially elementary school students, without having them in physically was a challenge for teachers. As I already indicated, students fell behind academically for two years.

Chapter 4

How the pandemic impacted parents, students, and teachers

Everybody was affected by the pandemic in one way or another. This section focuses on how the pandemic impacted parents, students, and teachers.

HOW THE PANDEMIC IMPACTED PARENTS

Parents and guardians are important partners in the education of their children. We have three types of parents: parents with adolescent children, parents with young children, and parents with disabled children. The first group of parents had the option of leaving the children at home and going to work. But the children's lack of motivation for school remained a major concern for these parents.

As for the second group of parents, the situation was more complicated: they could not leave their young children at home to go to work. Many parents lost their jobs and had to stay home with their children. These parents were obliged to stay closer to their children in order to help them take lessons from their computers. It was not easy for these parents to keep their children's concentration on the lessons. Some of these parents turned into teachers. Others were, sadly, lost because they couldn't remember the concepts taught to their children, and therefore could not help them with their assignments. In some cases, their difficulty in supervising their children was due to the change in teaching techniques.

The parents who have suffered the most are those with disabled children. Before the pandemic, these parents dropped off their children at school, and specialized teachers took care of them as best they could. With the pandemic and the shutdown, parents had to manage the behavior of their children with behavioral disorders all day long by themselves. These children sometimes have a very limited attention span. Those of them who were aggressive damaged the computer intended for their teaching.

The challenges some parents faced made them wonder if they were the teachers.

Parents with two or more children have struggled with space management at home, especially when their children would have to take classes virtually. The house turned into classrooms. During music lessons or physical education (PE), the noise level at home was not bearable.

HOW THE PANDEMIC IMPACTED STUDENTS

During the pandemic, students worked from home, which is a setting different from school. The school setting is more organized and well structured compared to the home setting. As already stated, many students were taking classes in their beds, half-dressed. They lacked interest in instruction. The shutdown imposed because of the pandemic deprived students of socialization: they could not meet each other in person and play together. The lack of socialization has caused depression and mental illness in some students.

Normally, students spend most of the day, about seven hours per day, with their teachers. During the shutdown, they spent the whole day with their parents. Some of these students were regularly abused by their parents.

Most of those students lost the motivation to learn. They procrastinated. They kept postponing the completion of their homework. The situation became so serious that some school districts extended the deadline to submit late assignments. After that deadline, some students still did not submit their homework. They then transferred the completion of their homework to their parents or siblings — and I've been seeing a rise of this in my classroom. In such cases, the good grades they received did not reflect reality, as I already mentioned. When those students returned in person to the campus, they seemed to have forgotten everything and could not achieve half of the grades they had previously received with help.

Many students lost their parents. Some of them lost both their parents and became orphans. In this painful situation, school was not their priority—their grief for their lost parents was. Imagine a child who was living joyfully with his parents, one had a lot of hope for the future but then suddenly became motherless, fatherless, and homeless! If you did not find yourself in such a situation, be grateful.

The only option some of those children had was to stay in a foster home. In most cases, those children were depressed. They developed mental health problems and dropped out of school or stayed under treatment. Some of them, unfortunately, committed suicide.

Overall, many students fell behind because of the pandemic. Students seemed to have lost interest in school during and after the pandemic.

HOW THE PANDEMIC IMPACTED TEACHERS

Teachers were burned out. The synchronous and asynchronous methods were new to them. They had to take training and work hard to master and use the new methods in a short period of time. One of the main challenges for teachers was classroom management online. They were physically far from their students, which made classroom management difficult. They had to deal with students who were making noise, and with some of their parents who were disturbing the class with music or conversation in the background.

Overall, students, parents, and teachers have been impacted by the pandemic in various ways. They all experienced emotional stress.

Chapter 5

Children yesterday and today

Have you heard people saying that we are the products of our environment? This is true for adults. It is also true for our children: they are the products of our society. When we compare children from yesterday with children today, it appears that children yesterday were not necessarily living in luxury. They barely had what they needed. But society was more organized with the education of those children. Parents took more responsibility for the education of their children. Members of society joined hands to educate kids.

In Africa, it is said that it takes a village to raise a child. Part of what this means is that everybody, not necessarily a biological parent, has the power to address any child's misbehavior. Children knew that nobody in society would tolerate their misbehavior. The only option they had was to be respectful to everybody, especially to adults. Unfortunately, things have changed for the worse. Today, if you attempt to correct a child in the street who is doing something wrong, it is at your own risk: their parents may come after you and even sue you.

CHILDREN TODAY ARE SPOILED

They seem to have more than what they need. Can you believe that some parents buy their children who are still at elementary school the latest version of the cell phone? When those parents are at work or at home, they are texting or calling their children during school hours. How can such a child focus on the instruction?

ALL START FROM HOME

Some families are very disciplined. They model good manners to their children and teach them how to behave in public. In other families, it is the opposite. The only language used at home is profanity. Children from such a family usually bring it to school. For them, it is fine to curse their classmates and even their teachers.

CHILDREN TODAY HAVE TOO MUCH POWER

Children today have too much power, and some of them are misusing it. We can agree that some parents abuse their children. Laws created to protect them must always be enforced. However, children are exposed to various instructions advising them to call the police when they are in danger. I have heard of students using this to their advantage when faced with discipline at home. While their parent or legal guardian did nothing wrong, trouble-making students call the authorities in a performance of tears and arrange for the wrongful arrest of their parents.

In some cases, those children are removed from their family and put in foster care. It is clear that life in foster care cannot be compared to life in the family.

Today teachers are fired just because they raised their voice while talking to a student.

The first part of this book sufficiently indicates that the educational system is like a seriously ill patient in need of urgent treatment. How to treat this great patient? The second part of this book constitutes adequate therapy for the problems.

PART 2

HOW TO SAVE THE EDUCATIONAL SYSTEM

This last part of the book constitutes suggestions for the issues which undermine the educational system

Chapter 6

Four days of school

During the school year, students spend most of their time with their teachers. They are in school for about 7 hours a day, or about 35 hours a week. Teachers are like substitutes for their parents.

For the sake of school innovation and to further galvanize teachers, it would be desirable to go from five school days a week to four school days. As mentioned above, students take an average of 35 hours of classes over five days, Monday through Friday. The change can be made in the following way: students may have an additional hour and a half of school per day, with two recesses. For example, instead of attending from 7:30 a.m. to 1:30 p.m., students may attend from 7:30 a.m. to 3 p.m. With the extension of the school day by an hour and a half per day, students may be in school from Monday to Thursday and have Friday off. Friday would be well indicated for the day off because it is the beginning of the weekend. Students and teachers may stay at home on Friday, Saturday, and Sunday.

There is a shortage of teachers. The school districts are desperately looking for teachers. Many teachers are in the classroom without qualification. Friday may be used for their training. Friday should be considered as a professional day. Professional development (PD) days for teachers are days teachers receive training to improve their performance. Teachers in some schools are required to complete at least 60 hours of PD per year. But it is optional in many schools. PD can take the form of a workshop, webinar, or conference: during the workshop, attendees participate in some specific activities. During the webinar, the speaker trains attendees on one topic. As far as the conference is concerned, many speakers teach on the same topic.

HOW TO ORGANIZE AN EFFICIENT PROFESSIONAL DEVELOPMENT (PD) DAY

Prior to PD, a survey should be sent to potential participants to identify their needs; this is important because the purpose of the PD is to provide solutions to problems teachers encounter. PD increases teachers' expertise in their field. PD can be in person or virtual. If it is in person, organizers should accommodate participants by making sure that the room has chairs, notebooks, pens, air conditioning, and a good sound system. If it is virtual, all participants must have a good internet connection.

The PD should focus on specific goals. During the PD, participants should have the opportunity to interact. Informal and formal assessments should be performed to evaluate the understanding of participants. The PD should be designed in a way to answer participants' questions or concerns. At the end of the PD, all participants should provide feedback: it helps organizers to know how the PD went and gives suggestions for future PD.

ADVANTAGES OF THE PD

PD allows teachers to learn new skills. It improves teachers' knowledge. Teachers learn new methods of teaching. Teachers who are well trained are more productive. They are more confident in teaching. PD prepares teachers to face challenges. During PD, teachers also have the opportunity to collaborate.

WHERE SHOULD PD TAKE PLACE?

In countries where the technology is not advanced, the PD must be done in person. In countries where technology is well advanced, the ideal is to do PD virtually: this allows teachers to work from home. They are thus spared fuel costs and transport risks.

HOW LONG SHOULD THE PD BE?

The PD and any other training should not exceed four hours. For the rest of the day, teachers should plan their lessons, grade assignments, and rest.

MENTORSHIP FOR NEWLY HIRED TEACHERS

Friday can be a good day to train newly hired teachers. Each new teacher should have a mentor teacher. Research indicates that when new teachers do not have a mentor who can train and motivate them, they resign in their first two years of teaching. This is more obvious with special education teachers who have to deal with a lot of paperwork. The mentor has the responsibility to coach the new teachers and help them meet their goals. The mentor teaches new teachers various teaching methods and provides them with advice to make them successful.

This innovation has several advantages: Friday off would allow teachers to rest better and have more time to correct homework and prepare lessons. With life becoming more and more expensive, the underpaid teacher can save gas by staying home on Fridays. Students will have enough time to review their lessons and complete their homework. Friday could be used for asynchronous instruction; students stay home but have enough assignments to be busy. They may complete those assignments at their own pace.

The option of four school days per week for students presents fewer problems for parents with teenagers because they are more responsible and can stay home alone. The problem is on the side of parents with very young children. They cannot leave their children alone at home. For parents who can work over the weekend and are able to take Friday off, it is a little easier to solve this dilemma. This is even easier to implement in Africa, where out of solidarity everyone takes care of the child, whether biological or not.

Overall, four days of school for students has more pros than cons. This change could also help improve the quality of education.

CHAPTER 7
No snow days

In some parts of the world, such as Africa, there are only two seasons: the dry season and the rainy season. Those areas are not concerned with snow. In other parts of the globe, there are four seasons: fall, winter, spring, and summer. During winter, there is snow.

Snow is made of ice crystals that suspend in the atmosphere, grow, and then fall. When it falls in great quantities, it creates an accumulation. The roofs of houses, trees, grass, and roads turn white. When it snows, it is cold, sometimes extremely cold. We are obliged to wear appropriate clothes. The frequency of snow varies from place to place. In areas with abundant snow, the community is prepared with equipment to clean it and allow activities to continue.

NO MORE SNOW DAYS

Snow can be dangerous. It may lead to power failure. Avalanches may occur in heavy snow. Staying in the snow without proper clothes may lead to death. Heavy snow may paralyze the whole city. Snow may cause traffic accidents.

A blizzard is a severe form of snow. When this happens, people are stuck in their homes, sometimes for days, without electricity and food if arrangements have not been made. Sleet is another form of snow. It does not necessarily create accumulation, but it can be very slippery and make the traffic dangerous.

School districts include snow days in their annual calendar. Very often, there is more snow than expected, which disrupts the originally established school calendar.

Schools should not be closed because of snow. Obviously, the safety of students and teachers should be the school priority; however, instead of closing schools and depriving students of classes, it would be desirable to retain the possibility of continuing the virtual classes without interruption, from home, thanks to Zoom links. This arrangement not only allows the continuity of lessons but also avoids late starts to summer break for students and teachers; otherwise, when there are more snow days than expected, students who stay home lose school days. In some cases, school districts are forced to extend the end of the school year to make up for lost days.

Students and teachers can stay home and still have the class virtually. School districts must be prepared for a future pandemic by reinforcing the schools with equipment that allows teachers and students to work from home in the event of an emergency situation. Instead of losing a day of instruction because of snow, school districts may keep the Google classroom with the Zoom links for synchronous learning: in this case teachers are teaching from the comfort of their home and students are at home. Students can receive direct feedback from their teachers. Another option is asynchronous teaching: teachers record and post assignments for students to complete while they are at home.

Chapter 8
Teach more, test less

WHAT IS A TEST?

For the purposes of this chapter, a test is a set of questions designed to measure someone's skill or knowledge in a specific area.

THE PURPOSE OF THE TESTING

The purpose of the testing is to assess students' level of performance in one or multiple subjects. The test indicates areas where students are struggling and informs the teacher about where to adjust the lesson to support those students.

Based on the test results, the teacher may create individualized lesson plans to meet the specific needs of students. The test results may also give the teacher an idea of the interventions to use to improve students' performance. Reading and math interventions include computer programs Iready, Dreambox, and Read 180, just to name a few. Students have to use those interventions daily with consistency to see the result.

With new technology, each principal is able to generate the school score and compare it with that of the whole district's expectation. The computer can create a graph indicating if a student is below or above the school's and the district's expectations.

TEST ANXIETY

The test does not always represent students' real level of knowledge. Some students have test anxiety that leads to poor performance. Test anxiety varies from student to student. Here are some signs of test anxiety: Some students sweat profusely before the test, including suffering from sweaty palms. Other students express a frequent desire for urination. They may ask to use the restroom before and during the test. Other students display a sudden shortage of breath. They breathe rapidly. Before the test, some students have nausea and even vomit. On the eve or on the test day, some students simulate a sickness to stay home. These issues disappear after the test.

HOW THE TEST ANXIETY IMPACTS STUDENTS' PERFORMANCE

Students who study want to do well in their tests. Some of them want to do so well that they end up being stressed out during the test and perform below their expectations. Test anxiety reduces students' performance. Students who suffer from it struggle to demonstrate their knowledge during the test; they lack focus and forget everything they have learned. The anxiety reduces students' confidence and makes them think they know nothing.

SOME TIPS TO ALLEVIATE TEST ANXIETY

The following strategies can help students reduce their test anxiety: they need to be confident and picture themselves as experts. Students must consider the test day not as a special day, but as an ordinary day. Putting too much importance on the test day makes some students nervous. Students must keep in mind that the test is an opportunity for them to show what they know.

The day before the test, students should get enough sleep. Good sleep helps the memory to rest and to recall what we have learned. Sleep can also improve mood. Students must develop self-control through relaxation and breathing techniques. They must eat and drink enough to have energy during the test. Being on time can also help students to be prepared. When they come late, they panic and lack focus during the test.

TEST RESULTS AS PART OF TEACHERS' EVALUATIONS

In many school districts, the test is part of the teacher's evaluation. Teachers can be fired if students have poor scores on standardized tests. Teachers are just as stressed as students during the test. To keep their job, they spend most of the time training students to pass the test. In such a situation, the only thing that matters for them is students' scores.

Different strategies can help students pass a test without necessarily having a good knowledge of the curriculum. Preparing students to pass the test becomes more important than implementing the curriculum.

Using students' test scores to assess teachers' performance is not fair. Although teachers have the responsibility to implement the curriculum, they have no control over the outcome of the test. We've seen situations where the best students had a bad score on the test and the average students scored well on the same test.

HOW TESTING IS IMPLEMENTED

Teachers are overwhelmed by tests. They are asked to test students regularly, sometimes as often as once per month. The length of a test can vary from one day to two weeks, depending on the school district. Let's suppose that students are tested every two months for one week. With nine months of school, the testing alone will take about four weeks of instructional time. That is a lot.

Teachers start and end the teaching cycle with less time for instruction. They spend more time administering that test. Teachers are dealing with classrooms that are more and more overcrowded. By the time they finish the testing, they are burned out.

TESTING LIMITATIONS

Testing alone is not enough to improve students' performance. If teachers are frequently testing students without teaching them, their performance may decrease instead of increase, or stay the same. It is just like someone who has $100 in their wallet. If they do not work to make more money, when they open that wallet, they will see the same $100. But if they work more, the $100 may become $200 or more.

Teachers must test less and teach more. At the beginning of the school year, teachers must perform a Beginning of Year (BOY) test to have an idea of the students' level. They must implement the curriculum and use any available interventions. They must use various instructional strategies including small groups or one-on-one instruction to support students. Parents at home must also support with homework to help students maintain good grades. In the middle of the school year, students must take the midyear test. If all strategies are well implemented, there is no reason students will not improve. Teachers will continue to teach and make students take the end of year (EOY) test. By doing so, teachers will complete all chapters included in the curriculum, with less stress and less pressure. Also, the length of each test must be reduced to two days maximum. The test results should be available as soon as possible to teachers and students. The outcome of testing must be used purposely. Testing students just as a formality is a waste of time.

Many countries in Africa need to improve the way students are assessed. In those countries, students take one test at the end of the school year. That test is crucial. If a student fails that test, they will repeat the class. Some students repeat their class for two and even three years because of that test. Such a test penalizes students; it is not fair. It does not necessarily match what was taught in the class. That test is not fair in that some students master what was taught all year long; they are even considered the best students, but they fail the test. When they fail, their parents pay the tuition again, because education is not free. Again, it is not fair for a student to repeat their class because they failed the end of year test; various factors affect the test score. A student may have poor performance on that test because they are going through some challenges such as the death of a family member or even some health issues. Some students fail the test not because they do not know the content, but because they are not good at using the technology, and that is not fair. If a student fails the test because that test involves typing with the computer, the question to ask is, are we testing students' knowledge of the content or technology? If we are testing the content knowledge of a student who has challenges typing, it may not be fair to have that student fail the class.

Overall, too many tests overwork teachers, limit the instruction, and therefore impact students' performance in a negative way.

CHAPTER 9
Teachers' motivation

Teachers are indispensable agents in the improvement of the educational system. Everyone in society has been taught by a teacher. Teachers need to be motivated in several ways for effective change.

TEACHERS' RESPECT AS A MOTIVATING FACTOR

Before, the teacher was considered a master; that is to say, someone who masters, who knows. Teachers were highly respected in society, and rightly so: they are the ones who taught everyone in society, including the leaders of this world. Why did everything change?

Today, teachers are not well respected. Some students talk to their teachers as they want and even attack them, without consequence. Some parents disrespect teachers and prevent them from doing their job correctly. It is common to have some parents cursing teachers over the phone. Some of those parents go to the school and curse a teacher in front of their colleagues and students. I guess some parents think of cursing their children's teacher as a "reward" for serving their community. Teachers are sometimes ridiculed by their boss, through an unjustified bad evaluation or verbal aggression. Lack of respect for teachers forces many to quit their jobs. This may be one of the reasons for the teachers shortage.

Overall, teachers must be respected. A student can hurt a teacher with no consequence. A parent can curse a teacher with no consequence, but the opposite is not possible. If a teacher curses a parent, the teacher is fired. A teacher can be fired if they raise their voice while correcting a student who is doing something wrong. However, those who make decisions impacting teachers are not teachers. They work in the office, and most of the time they are disconnected from the reality in the classroom. Teachers should be involved in decision making. They should provide their input for any change in school.

TEACHERS' SALARY AS MOTIVATION

Give teachers the salary they deserve. The question prospective teachers ask themselves is: why burn myself out for a hard, less-paying job when I can expend less energy on another job for more money?

Respected and well-paid teachers are more motivated and tend to take better care of their students. In comparison with other professions, teachers are underpaid. Most of them complete their education with a mountain of student loan debt to pay. Some teachers are obliged to have a second job in order to pay their bills.

In many competitive schools, only teachers with at least a bachelor's or a master's degree are hired. To complete their education, those teachers take out student loans. When they graduate, they have a mountain of debt to pay. The monthly minimum payment of that debt is an important portion of their salary. They cannot afford to buy a nice car or house because they are broke. Everyone in society, regardless of social rank, has been educated by teachers. But why are they so neglected?

Teaching pays less than other professions. A teacher who has a master's degree in education is paid less than someone who has an associate degree with just some information technology (IT) certifications. The teacher trains the students in almost all areas, but these students earn more money than the teacher. What a teacher earns is not proportional to the work they do: They prepare lessons until late hours, teach all day, and correct homework even during the weekends and holidays. Between classes, they participate in meetings and training. All day long, they suffer the whims of the students. The motivation of the teacher can increase if they earn a high salary.

Pay teachers, pay them more, give them what they deserve. Yes, give them what they deserve. Teachers are becoming increasingly rare; many of them quit. Few people want to join this profession. One of the ways to enhance teaching is to change the salary scale of teachers and make this profession the best-paid profession, and we will have more teachers and quality teaching.

CHANGE IN TEACHERS' EVALUATIONS AS A MOTIVATING FACTOR

Regularly, teachers are observed and evaluated. That is a good idea because the evaluation helps to identify those who are doing a great job and those who are struggling. A teacher whose performance is below expectations can become a wonderful teacher if they receive more training and support. The current evaluation system needs to be improved because it puts more stress on teachers.

Teachers' evaluations have an impact on their salary and job retention. It is not fair because a 30-minute observation by a school principal does not always capture the whole of a teacher's performance. Generally, anyone who is observed ceases to be natural, and this leads to underperformance. Some students, coincidentally, choose that day to misbehave and may make the observer give the teacher a bad grade for lack of class management.

Some school principals use teachers' evaluations as a means of retaliation. The evaluation is subjective. A teacher can be good but receive a poor grade and vice versa. It is possible for a principal to give a poor grade to a teacher and use it to get rid of them. Teachers contesting their evaluation have small chance to reverse the score received. They may involve the teachers union, but in most cases, they lose the case, which is not fair. I am a victim of that unfair evaluation. I suffered from it.

Chapter 10

Home school as an alternative to traditional schools

Homeschooling is becoming an alternative to traditional school. What justifies the change? What is needed to start a home school? What are the advantages and the limitations of homeschooling? These questions and more will be answered in this chapter.

WHAT IS HOMESCHOOLING?

Homeschooling has various synonyms and variations: home-based education, home education, unschooling, home-centered learning, home instruction, and deschooling (Luebke, 1999; Taylor, 1986 b). There is no standard definition of homeschooling. Murphy (2012) made a compilation of homeschooling definitions, as shown below.

Homeschooling has been described as:

- "a teaching situation wherein children learn in the home in lieu of a conventional school. The parents, tutors, or guardians assume the direct responsibility for the education of their children." (Taylor, 1986 b, p.14)

- "a school conducted in the home by a parent primarily for the education of the children in that home." (Glading, 1987, P.12)

- an "instruction and learning, at least some of which is through planned activity, taking place primarily at home in a family setting with a parent acting as a teacher or supervisor of the activity, and with one or more pupils who are members of the same family and who are doing grade K–12 work." (Line, 1991, p.10)

- "the education of school-aged children under their parents' general monitoring, and it replaces full-time attendance at a campus school." (Line, 1991. p.1)

- "the practice of educating children and youth during what most people call the elementary and secondary school years, in learning environment that is home based and parent-led (or, at least, clearly under the authority of the parent rather than under the authority of a state-run public school system or private school.)" (Ray, 2004a. P. 3)

- "an alternative form of education in which children are instructed at home rather than a traditional public or private school. The children who are homeschooled are instructed by parents, guardians, or other tutors" (Lips & Feinberg, 2008, p. 2).

"Homeschoolers are predominantly white and middle class, many espouse conservative protestant faiths; their households have full-time or nearly full-time moms." (Stevens, 2001, pp. 17–18)

WHY IS HOMESCHOOLING GROWING?

Due to the shutdown during the COVID-19 pandemic, there were no incidents on campuses; everybody was at home. But as soon as students physically returned to their campuses, their fights were recorded here and there. Bullying and shooting in schools resumed. This makes parents think about homeschooling.

In support of homeschooling, some parents argue that the traditional schools do not take into consideration their religion and expose students to some concepts that are not good but that have been made politically correct, or else schools impose what students have to learn regardless of their religions. Not all that is asked of students today respects their beliefs. In traditional schools, parents are limited in the ways they can teach their children what they believe.

Violence in traditional schools has become a persistent source of fear affecting the daily lives of students, teachers, and parents. Students are killing other students and teachers with guns. Criminals are easily entering school buildings to kill innocent students, sometimes for unknown reasons. Shootings in schools create chaos. The school can be closed for a couple of days for investigation; it will end up opening with the risk of having the same issue because the root of the problem is not addressed properly.

Many parents are reluctant to expose their children to what is happening at schools today. That includes excess freedom given to students to do what they want, most of the time without consequences. It seems to be okay for a student to insult the teacher in the classroom or to throw objects at them during the instruction because students know they will not be suspended or expelled. Students who are well educated are frustrated when they see what has happened, and if they have a choice, they will quit that environment.

In most parts of the world, the school setting is dangerous because students are being exposed to all kinds of drugs. The situation is so serious that some students are drug dealers. In sum, the expansion of homeschooling is partially justified by the failure of the traditional school.

WHAT IS NOT HOMESCHOOLING?

Allie-Carson (1990) stressed that the choice of home school, refusing traditional schooling, must be voluntary. In other words, there should be no constraint. Aurini and Davies (2005) indicated that if a student receives instruction at home because they cannot go to school, that is not considered as homeschooling. Students who receive education at home because of their medical condition are not homeschoolers (Belfield, 2004, Princiotta, Bielick and Chapman, 2004). Knowles and Muchmore (1995) mentioned that students who are learning from home because their parents have opted to travel are not homeschoolers.

BRIEF HISTORY OF HOMESCHOOLING

Homeschooling is not new. Isenberg (2007) indicated that a religious group started homeschooling in the 1970s. Later on, its evolution was affected by Jean-Jacques Rousseau's philosophy. Many legal battles took place and ended up with the legalization of homeschooling in 1990 in the USA. Isenberg (2007) found that in 2007 there were about a million homeschoolers, the equivalent of the combination of charter schools and voucher schools.

Ray (2022) found that in the United States, for the academic year 2021/2022, there were 3.135 million homeschoolers in grades K–12. This confirms the growing population of homeschoolers. The two years of the COVID-19 pandemic sped up the growth of homeschooling.

WHAT DOES IT TAKE TO START A HOME SCHOOL?

It is suggested that among those who opted for homeschooling, at least one parent should stay home. In general, families who choose homeschooling for their children are well educated. The requirements to start a home school vary from country to country and from state to state. It is strongly encouraged that parents considering homeschooling thoroughly research the requirements in their own locale.

LIMITATIONS OF HOMESCHOOLING

Homeschooling has some limitations: students miss socialization because they are not in contact with other students in traditional schools. Homeschooling requires financial sacrifices from parents. One parent may give up their job to stay home. In some cases, parents may have to redesign their house to make it look like a school, and that involves a cost. There is not enough space at a typical home to play sports compared to the traditional school with a gymnasium. Students with disabilities may miss some of their services, such as speech therapy or occupational therapy. Home schools do not provide nursing services. In case of an emergency, parents may have to call the hospital directly. Homeschooling may not receive school funding from the government.

ADVANTAGES OF HOMESCHOOLING

Students in home school follow a flexible schedule with various advantages: it is easy for their parents to make a doctor's appointment for them. They are able to pause the instruction when they are not ready to learn. Students have the full attention of teachers because the model of instruction is "one on one." Teachers have enough time to make sure that students understand the concepts taught. Homeschooling builds more connection between parents and children because they spend more time together.

I am suspecting that if the traditional school continues to fail, in the long run homeschooling may dominate and traditional school buildings will be half-empty.

Chapter 11
Other Recommendations

ABOUT BULLYING

Bullying in school is becoming a serious concern. Some students are dropping out of school because of bullying. What can be done to prevent or alleviate bullying? Students must be trained to self-advocate. Some victims do not have the courage to tell what happened to them; they should be able to report such an incident as soon as it happens.

Don't we say that prevention is better than cure? The emphasis should be on the prevention of bullying and not on its consequences. Students need more supervision during breakfast, lunch, recess, and dismissal. At those times, the incidence of bullying is high.

Schools should be able to identify what triggers bullying. Surprisingly, some students bully others just because they are bored. A well-structured classroom and solid instruction may limit or prevent bullying.

For when bullying does occur, the school must implement a zero-tolerance policy. Those who bully should be suspended as a first warning. If they become repeat offenders, they should be permanently expelled from the school. Some people may think that such a decision is excessive. They need to understand the seriousness of the problem: some students commit suicide because they are being bullied; others are traumatized for the rest of their lives.

ABOUT SCHOOL PRINCIPALS' POWER

Excessive power is given to school principals. Some have the right to fire a teacher, with or without a valid reason. A principal and a teacher may not get along, but this should not give the principal the opportunity to retaliate against the teacher. Some principals do this in a subtle way; others take advantage of an occasion, such as a fault committed by a teacher, to fire them. This clearly means that the teacher is not protected.

Firing a teacher should come from a decision of a committee made up of the teacher, the principal, the superintendent, and the teachers' union, which acts like a lawyer for the teacher.

ABOUT FAMILIES' PARTICIPATION

As I have already said, many parents have abandoned the education of their children to the teachers. They wrongly believe that it is the teacher who must do everything for their children. Real education begins at home, with the student's family. Some ungrateful parents will call the teacher to insult them on the pretext that they do not do their job well, unaware that it is rather the family's job.

The parents must provide the basis of education to their children. They must spend precious time with their children. Reading a children's book every evening with a child who is not yet of school age already prepares children for understanding; having them listen to an educational song for children every evening is recommended; but leaving the child for more than three hours watching television is to destroy the brain of the child. Parents must make an effort to understand their children, support them in their duties, and collaborate with teachers.

ABOUT SAFETY IN SCHOOL

It is difficult to determine how many students die every year in school from shooting or from any type of violence. Schools are getting less and less secure, and this is getting worrying. If it is not violence, it is drugs that dictate the law in the school environment.

Given the gravity of the situation, all schools without exception should be equipped with metal detectors: they can help to identify guns or any other weapon. Before entering school, students, teachers, and visitors should be searched for security purposes. Everyone should participate in making the school safe by alerting the police or school administration to any suspicious cases. Each school should have at least one behavior specialist, whose role is to act promptly to stop a fight before it escalates. The specialist also manages students' behavior to prevent some misbehavior issues.

Drug use or trafficking in and around schools should be strictly prohibited. The police or school administration should also be alerted when there is suspicion or evidence of drug use in the school environment. The success of securing schools is a job involving everyone.

ABOUT DEPARTMENTALIZATION

Simply explained, departmentalization means that academic subjects are regrouped into departments. For example, we have the science department, the English department, and so on. Teachers in the same department should regularly collaborate. They may share various teaching strategies and even their lesson plans. The innovation is to have each teacher teach only one specific subject.

Not all teachers are good at all subjects. The advantage is that the teacher who specializes in one area teaches the subject more effectively. The obstacle to this departmentalization is the shortage of teachers. However, if governments are serious about solving educational problems, they can find ways to recruit teachers and make such a proposal possible.

ABOUT MORALS IN SCHOOL

In the past, prayers and morals were taught in class as subjects in various countries. For political reasons, religion was first removed from school and morals followed. Morals helped to prepare students as good citizens.

Thanks to the teaching of morals, students were more able to exercise self-restraint. Morals taught students how to behave. Peace taught through morals could help to reduce violence and bullying in school. Morals taught students to respect each other and to respect teachers. Since the suppression of morals as a subject, students do not respect themselves, and they do not respect the teachers who teach them.

ABOUT TEACHER RETENTION

The shortage of teachers is a serious problem. Teachers are leaving teaching for other professions, and this will continue if nothing is done. In countries where dictatorship reigns, members of the military earn big salaries to protect the tyrant, but the teachers who educate everyone in society are underpaid and treated with disrespect. As long as this situation lasts, potential teachers will withdraw and move on to other professions.

To keep teachers and attract new people to teaching, it is absolutely necessary to substantially increase their salaries, give them more benefits, make the school environment more secure, and restore their respect.

ABOUT THE AMERICAN STUDENT LOAN CRISIS

America is one of the countries in the world where education at the higher levels is extremely expensive. Paradoxically, it is also one of the richest countries in the world. Studies at the university level seem to be discriminatory; they are more reserved for the rich. Students who are poor finish their studies early; if they absolutely want to go further, they have to take out a student loan. At the end of their studies, they find themselves with a mountain of debt and very high interest to pay.

The concept of student loans is unfair because the state has the means to make education free, or cheaper at all levels. America can copy the example of Germany, where students can go as far as they wish and finish their studies without debt. The pure and simple cancellation of this debt, and the change of the system to make access to studies easy for all, constitutes a solution to this student debt crisis.

CONCLUSION

When I started writing this book, I did not have any idea about how it would end. By reading from the first to the last chapter, you have indicated some interest in the content. If we can now agree that the education system is facing serious issues that need to be fixed, we should be part of the solution, not part of the problem.

Here are some questions to ask yourself: As a student, am I doing what I am supposed to do, for example, completing my assignments and homework? Am I peaceful and respectful? As a parent, am I supporting my children with their homework and collaborating with their teachers? As a teacher, am I preparing and delivering my lessons correctly? Am I following the school ethics? Am I collaborating with everyone, including families, students, colleagues, and staff? As a staff member, am I treating my colleagues fairly and respectfully? As a member of the community, what am I doing to stop bullying and any type of violence in school? As a politician, beyond speeches, what are we doing to stop shooting in school? Is there any level of gun violence against teachers and students in our schools that we are willing to accept as inevitable? Is it impossible to control guns and reinforce safety in schools?

Why should students waste school days because of snow when the Zoom or the asynchronous option could be used to continue instruction at home? Teachers are important agents of education; they should be respected and receive the salary they deserve for their hard work. Their voice should be heard. They should test students less and have more time for teaching. They must constantly receive training to remain effective. Overall, the school system should be made in a way to create good citizens well prepared to develop their community.

The final question everyone should ask is, "What am I doing at my level to make the school system better?"

References

Allie-Carson, J. (1990). Structure and interaction patterns of home school families. *Home school researcher,* 6(3), 11–18.

Aurini, J., & Davies, S. (2005). Choice without markets: Homeschooling in the context of private education. *British Journal of Sociology of Education, 26, 461–474.*

Belfield, C. (2004 a). *Home-schooling in the US* (Occasional Paper No. 88). New York: Columbia University, Teachers College, National Center for the Study of Privatization in Education.

Isenberg, E. (2007). What have we learned about homeschooling? *Peabody Journal of Education,* 82, 387–409.

Gillett. T. (2022). Cultivating new paradigms in mental health. *Cambridge Prisms: global mental health.* https://www.cambridge.org/core/blog/2022/12/12/cultivating-new-paradigms-in-mental-health/

Glading, E. (1987). Home education: Characteristics of its Families and schools (Unpublished doctoral dissertation). Bob Jones University, Greenville, SC.

Juvonen, J., & Graham, S. (2014). Bullying in Schools: The power of bullies and the plight of victims. *The Annual Review of Psychology.* https://bottemabeutel.com/wp-content/uploads/2014/01/Bullying-in-School.pdf

Kendi, I. X. (2019). *How to be anti-racist.* New York: One World.

Knowles, J. G., & Muchmore, J. A. (1995). Yep! We're grown-up home-schooled kids-and we're doing just fine, thank you. *Journal of Research on Christian Education,* 4(1), 35–56.

Lines, P. M. (1991). Home instruction: The size and growth of the movement. In J. van Galen & M. Pittman (Eds), *Homeschooling: political, historical, and pedagogical perspectives* (pp. 9–42). Norwood, NJ: Able.

Lips, D., & Feinberg, E. (2008). Homeschooling: A growing option in American Education. Washington, DC: Heritage Foundation.

Lubke, R. V. (1999). Homeschooling in Wisconsin: A review of current issues and trends. Milwaukee: Wisconsin Policy Research Institute.

Murphy, J. (2012). *Homeschooling in America: Capturing and assessing the movement.* Thousand Oaks, CA: Sage.

New Jersey Department of Education. "Strengthening Gifted and Talented Education Act," (2020), New Jersey. https://www.nj.gov/education/standards/gifted/docs/GiftedTalentedLegislation-Chapter%20338.pdf

Olweus, D. (1994). "Bullying at school: Basic facts and effects of a school-based intervention program," *Journal of Child Psychology and Psychiatry*, 35, no. 7: 1171-1190.

Princiotta, D. Bielick, S., & Chapman, C. (2004).*1.1 million homeschooled students in the United in 2003.* Washington, DC: National Center for Education Statistics

Ray, B. (2004 a). *Home educated and now adults: Their community and civic involvement, views about homeschooling, and other traits.* Salem, OR: National Home Education Research Institute.

Ray, B. D. (2022). *How many homeschool students are there in the United States during the 2021–2022 school year?* National Home Education Research Institute. Retrieved from https://www.nheri.org/how-many-homeschool-students-are-there-in-the-united-states-during-the-2021-2022-school-year

Rosales, J., and Walker, T. (2021). *The racist beginnings of the standardized testing.* National Education Association (NEA). Retrieved from https://www.nea.org/advocating-for-change/new-from-nea/racist-beginnings-standardized-testing

Shurkin, J. (1992). *Terman's kids: The groundbreaking study of how the gifted grow up.* New York: Little, Brown.

Scott-Clayton, J. E. (2018). The looming student loan crisis is worse than we thought. *Evidence Speaks 2(34)*. https://academiccommons.columbia.edu/doi/10.7916/D8WT05QV

Stevens, M. L. (2001). *Kingdom of children: Culture and controversy in the homeschooling movement.* Princeton, NJ: Princeton University Press.

Taylor, J. (1986 b). Self-concept in home-schooling children. *HomeSchool Research,* 2(2), 1–3.

U.S. Department of Education, National Center of Education Statistics (2021) *The Condition of Education (NCES 1021–144).*